Papier Mâché

and HOW TO USE IT

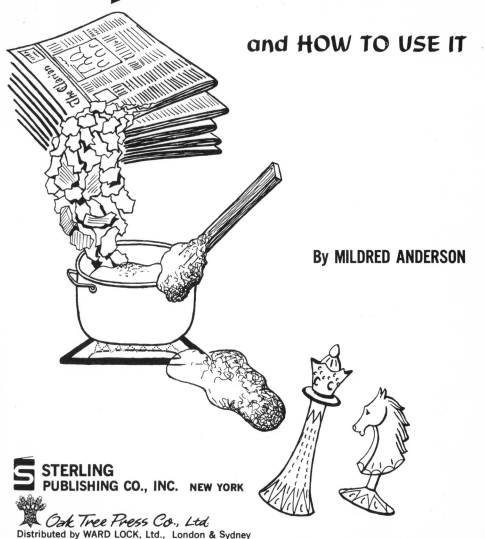

By MILDRED ANDERSON

STERLING PUBLISHING CO., INC. NEW YORK

Oak Tree Press Co., Ltd.
Distributed by WARD LOCK, Ltd., London & Sydney

STERLING CRAFTS BOOKS

Block & Silk Screen Printing

Cardboard Crafting

Carpentry for Children

Ceramics—and How to Decorate Them

Craft of Woodcuts

Creating from Scrap

Creative Claywork

Creative Embroidery

Creative Enamelling & Jewelry-Making

Creative Leathercraft

Creative Paper Crafts in Color

Designs—And How to Use Them

How to Make Things Out of Paper

Knitting Without Needles

Make Your Own Mobiles

Making Mosaics

Original Creations with Papier Mâché

Papier Mâché—and How to Use It

Plastic Foam for Arts and Crafts

Printing as a Hobby

Prints—from Linoblocks and Woodcuts

Sculpture for Beginners

Stained Glass Crafting

Tin-Can Crafting

Types of Typefaces

Weaving as a Hobby

PICTURE CREDITS

The back cover photograph, showing the author in the first stages of making a papier mâché lampshade, is by Michael Gilligan. The front cover photograph and all photographs used throughout the book are by Bob Carmichael-Moore.

Eighth Printing, 1970

Copyright © 1965 by
Sterling Publishing Co., Inc.
419 Park Avenue South, New York, N.Y. 10016
British edition published by Oak Tree Press Co., Ltd.
Distributed in Great Britain and the Commonwealth by
Ward Lock, Ltd., 116 Baker Street, London W1
Manufactured in the United States of America
All rights reserved
Library of Congress Catalog Card No.: 64-24685
ISBN 0-8069-5068-4   UK 7061 2021 3
5069-2

Contents

INTRODUCTION 5
1. THE RAW MATERIALS OF PAPIER MÂCHÉ 6
Paper 6
The Grain of Paper 6
Pastes and Glues 7
Other Materials 7
2. GETTING ACQUAINTED WITH PAPIER MÂCHÉ 8
Nut Dish 10
Salad Bowl 17
Salad Fork and Serving Spoon 19
3. PUTTING YOUR SKILLS TO WORK 23
Round Wastepaper Basket 23
Cylindrical Lampshades 24
Round Trays 26
Rectangular Trays 27
Rectangular Trays with Dividers 28
Sectional Shelves 30
Hat Boxes 32
4. FOLDED AND ROLLED OBJECTS 34
Beads 34
Buttons 37
Blinds 39
Woven Wastepaper Baskets 41
Cherubs and Figurines 43

5. THE ART OF WORKING WITH MASH 45
   How to Make Mash 45
   Round Bowl 48
   Flower Pot Covers 50
   Napkin Rings 51
   Cleansing Tissue Box Cover 52
   Child's Stool and Toy Box 53
   Rectangular Boxes with Lids and Lips 54
   Pencil Cups 58
   Spice and Condiment Canisters 60
   Shakers 63
   Funnels 65
   Panels 67
   Tool Box 68
   Lampshades 69
   Clock Case 70
   Puppet Heads 71
   Candlesticks 72
   Chess Table and Chessmen 75
   Nativity Scene 80
6. DRYING THE THINGS YOU MAKE 87
   Baking 87
7. DECORATING THE THINGS YOU MAKE 88
   Punching, or Incising 88
8. FINISHES FOR THE THINGS YOU MAKE 90
   Linseed Oil 90
   Opaque Finishes 91
   Transparent Finishes 92
9. PROJECTS FOR DAMP DAYS 94
   Whisk 94
   Supports for Drying 94
INDEX 96

Introduction

Papier mâché (the name literally means "chewed-up paper") has probably been known for as long as the art of paper-making has existed—for at least 2,000 years. Your local art museum may have some examples of papier mâché dating back many years. As recently as the Victorian period, a variety of household articles, including some pieces of furniture, were made from it.

Now, with modern advances in technology, new vistas have been opened up for the worker in papier mâché. Using various synthetic glues and such finishing materials as epoxy resins, it is now possible to create—from ordinary paper—objects that will be almost indestructible. Epoxy makes papier mâché objects virtually unbreakable, water-proof, flame-proof, burn-proof, alcohol- and acid-proof, stain-proof and soil-proof. Wiping with a damp cloth is all that is needed to keep epoxy-coated objects clean. Of course, you can protect papier mâché with a coating of the traditional materials— lacquer, shellac, paint or varnish finishes—and this book tells you how. But epoxy coatings, whose application is also described in detail in this book, does more than finish papier mâché articles; epoxy enters into the papier mâché and strengthens it.

If you can bake a cake or saw a board, you can make beautiful and enduring things with papier mâché. Many different methods have been worked out for you and are described in this book. Once you have learned them, you can start experimenting on your own.

What can you make? Choose anything from the projects that follow. Every object here has been made by me—a craft-minded amateur—in this Epoxy Age. These objects will stand up for a good long time. You, too, can make any of these objects without difficulty. Let this book show you how.

1. The Raw Materials of Papier Mâché

PAPER

The basic papier mâché raw material that you will use is paper. Of course, old newspapers will be your chief source of materials. However, you should not hesitate to experiment with other types of paper as a raw material. For example, business correspondence and records are traditionally on rag paper—which is paper made in part from rags, usually cotton or linen. The addition of the longer fibres of cotton or linen to the paper gives it strength and durability far exceeding that of paper made only from wood pulp.

Used fine stationery, old ledgers, bank and business records, drawing papers and damaged books may all be good sources of rag paper. Start collecting quality papers for use in special projects—such as gifts for special people—and you will be surprised how quickly your supply of quality papers will grow.

As you work with the newspapers that are available in your locality, you may find that the paper used in them (called "newsprint" in the trade) varies from newspaper to newspaper. Before long you may even develop preferences for the quality of the paper in one newspaper over another.

THE GRAIN OF PAPER

During the paper-making processes that transform the various vegetable fibres into what we know as "paper," the finished product acquires a certain pattern of fibre—called "grain." The easiest way to determine the grain of a particular piece of paper is to tear it.

Take an ordinary sheet of any newspaper. Tear it in the direction in which the columns of type run. Notice how it shreds, whether raggedly or evenly, and whether it tears easily. Now tear it in the other direction—across the columns. Notice how it shreds in this direction and compare the ease or difficulty of tearing. (This tearing of newspaper will also give you the "feel" of the paper.) You will find that it does indeed tear more easily in one direction—with the grain. Tearing the paper with the grain, you found that the tears were nice and even; in the other direction—against the grain—the tears were undoubtedly ragged, uneven and difficult to control. In general, you will find from your own experience that paper strips torn with the grain are stronger than the same-sized strips torn against the grain.

PASTES AND GLUES

Although you can mould objects from strips or lumps of moistened newspaper (and such objects would be reasonably firm), the addition of even a small amount of paste or glue will give the things you make added strength and permanence. In preparation for each of the papier mâché projects that follow, it is always a good idea to make a fresh batch of paste-glue mixture to the following formula:

½ cup of flour
¼ cup of powdered resin glue
one pint of water

Mix this thoroughly, adding the flour and powdered glue to the water a little at a time. Stir the mixture frequently with a wire coat hanger whisk (see page 94). The objective is to get a smooth, even mixture with no lumps or air bubbles.

OTHER MATERIALS

The only other materials that you will need to get started in making papier mâché objects are a large cooking pot, a plastic bucket, a couple of baking sheets and some fancy papers (gift-wrapping papers are good)—that's about all.

2. Getting Acquainted with Papier Mâché

In making objects of papier mâché, you will use two basic methods: In the early projects you will build up objects around a mould, using paste-coated strips of paper. Later you will learn to make objects from the pulpy mass of boiled paper called "mash."

One final word of advice before you begin: Accompanying each project is a "materials checklist" that describes the materials you will need to assemble for that project. Be sure that you have all of them before you begin. It could be frustrating to have to look for some critically needed material while the paste is drying. You should also read and then re-read the instructions carefully, studying the illustrations as you go along. Make sure that you understand exactly what you are going to do before you begin a project. If you are not certain how to proceed at a certain point, study the step-by-step diagrams or the illustrations of the object to see exactly what you are trying to achieve.

Many of the things that you will make will be made over or around a mould. Do not think of this as "cheating." Because of the nature of paper and in particular because of the relatively large quantity of water used during the papier mâché making, objects of papier mâché have a strong tendency to warp—often differentially. A mould, therefore, is a "must" —particularly for beginning projects. After you have learned how to handle papier mâché and to know its qualities, you can dispense with moulds and create papier mâché objects without them. The things that you make then may even seem twisted and crooked, but this will only add to their uniqueness and charm.

The moulds that you use will be determined by the nature of the article that you are making. All kinds of wooden and cardboard boxes may be used; dishes make excellent moulds for rounded objects. Anything with sides sloping in toward the bottom is good—there will be no problem in removing the object you have made. For deep things, like a wastepaper basket, a few layers of newspaper should cover the mould before you build up the papier mâché.

8

Illus. 1. This attractive file box measures
9 x 12 x 12 inches and was made to
accommodate standard file holders.

Some objects may be difficult to remove from their moulds; if you en-
counter difficulty, make a small hole in the moulded papier mâché piece
and this will "release" the vacuum. Patch the hole you have made with
paste-coated strips of paper after the piece has been removed from the
mould.

One-half-inch wire mesh offers possibilities for exploration in the creation
of moulds for papier mâché articles. Because of the air spaces in the mesh,
papier mâché articles made on mesh moulds dry quickly and thoroughly.
And the finished work lifts easily off the mould every time.

NUT DISH

Illus. 2

Your first project will be to make a papier mâché nut dish, using a glass, plastic or china salad or breakfast-food bowl as a mould.

Materials Checklist
stack of newspapers
2-quart container (plastic or aluminium)
flour and powdered resin glue mixture (see page 7)
glass, plastic or china salad or breakfast-food bowl
emery paper
raw linseed oil
black brushing lacquer

Begin by covering the table or work space with about a dozen layers of newspaper to absorb excess water and to protect the surface.

Take a thick section of newspaper from your stack of newspapers (not a tabloid paper, however). Tear this at the middle fold into two sections of single pages. Tear these in half and then into quarters. Tear along the outside, or cut edges, of the pieces so that a thin strip is removed, leaving all edges as "feather" edges.

Make one pile of your torn sheets. Place these on your work table alongside the sink or a pan of water.

Shuffle about two dozen of the torn newspaper sheets into the sink or pan of water, one sheet at a time. The idea is to get them into the water in a random fashion so that the edges are not together and so that the sheets will be easier to pick up individually.

Take the wet newspaper sheets from the water and place them next to the bowl.

Spread some of the flour-resin glue mixture on the top sheet. Use your hand for this; if you dip your hand about halfway into the paste mixture, this should take up just the right amount of paste. Tear this sheet in half in your hand. Place the two halves together and tear in half again in the same direction to make one laminated strip composed of four individual strips of newspaper joined by thin layers of paste with none of the four edges exactly together. (See Illustration 3.) *Learn this technique*—you will use it in many of the projects in this book.

Place this strip on the bowl through the middle, paste side out. Repeat this process, adding strips through the middle to make a star-like pattern on the bowl. (See Illustration 3.) Tearing the paper in your hand to make laminated strips will enable the building-up process to go along about four times as fast as it would by adding single thickness strips.

Each time you place the strips on the mould, press them tightly from the middle outwards. This will remove any air pockets, lumps of paste, or excess water. Your finished dish will be harder and stronger as a result. *This pressing is a necessity if you want strong papier mâché.*

Repeat the tearing of a paste-covered sheet as before to make a laminated strip. Apply this paste side down in the middle, so that it is parallel to your body. Follow this with other paste-side-down strips all running in the same direction. (See Illustration 4.) Cover the entire dish in this way.

Now do the same, covering the dish with strips applied perpendicular to your body. These, of course, will also be at right angles to the layer of strips you have just applied and will be paste side down. (See Illustration 5.)

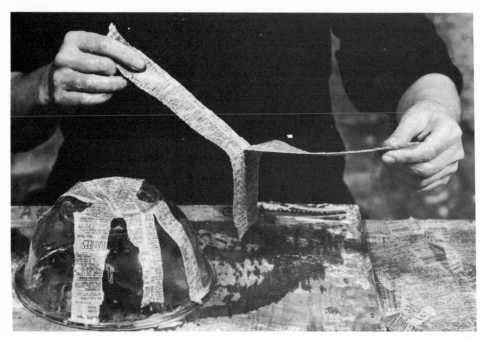

Illus. 3. Tear the paste-covered paper into strips and apply the strips in a star pattern to the bowl serving as a mould.

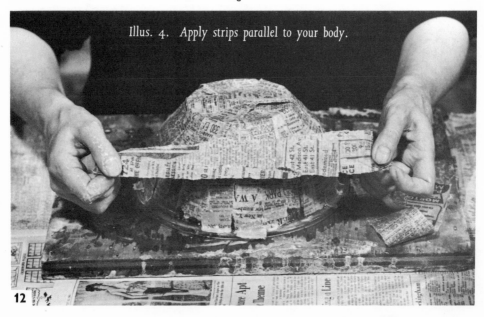

Illus. 4. Apply strips parallel to your body.

Illus. 5. Apply strips at right angles to your body.

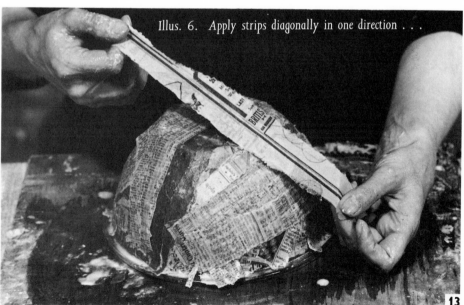

Illus. 6. Apply strips diagonally in one direction . . .

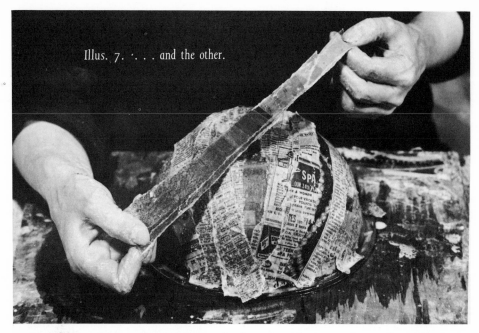

Illus. 7. ·. . . and the other.

Only the first layer of strips is applied paste side up to keep the object you are making from sticking to the mould.

Next, apply strips diagonally, first in one direction (Illustration 6) and then in the other (Illustration 7).

The edges of your papier mâché dish will be thinner than the rest of the piece, because many of the strips will not completely reach the edge. This concentration of strips and the resulting increased thickness will give strength in the base of your dish—where it is needed—without the appearance of heaviness elsewhere. However, if you want the edge of your papier mâché dish to be thicker, you can always build it up with additional strips of paper.

When your papier mâché dish has reached the thickness that you want, remove the bowl that has been serving as a mould. The top edge of your papier mâché dish will be ragged, but leave it this way for now.

You may now handle the papier mâché dish without fear of damaging it. Turn the mould and dish right side up. Remove your dish from the mould. Press across the bottom of the papier mâché dish and up the sides

Illus. 8. Trim the ragged edge of the papier mâché bowl with scissors.

to squeeze any excess water, paste or air bubbles to the edges and out of the dish entirely.

Bake it on a baking sheet thinly coated with raw linseed oil in an oven that has been pre-heated to 250°. (The coating of linseed oil will ensure that your dish does not stick to the baking sheet.) In from 5 to 10 minutes, your papier mâché dish should be "done" enough for you to continue working on it.

Remove it from the oven and trim the ragged edge with a pair of scissors. (See Illustration 8.) First mark a straight line all round with a pencil and cut along this. Don't worry about how thin the edge of your dish may be after you have trimmed it.

Check the dish for sturdiness, thickness, smoothness and stiffness. Press the sides with the palms of your hands. If the dish bends at all under pressure, it is not thick enough; more papier mâché strips will have to be added in the thin or weak spots and the piece re-baked. A soft spot on the surface means an air pocket or bubble underneath. If you find such an air pocket, cut an X-incision into the air pocket from the inside of the dish.

15

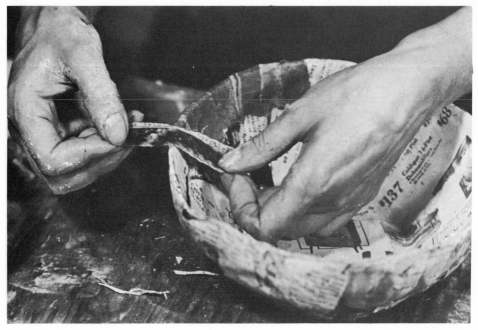

Illus. 9. Apply short paste-covered strips to build up the thin edge of the papier mâché bowl.

Press some of the paste mixture into the pocket and cover it with one or more four-layer patches larger in area than the X-incision, pressing very hard, as always.

Cover the edge of the papier mâché dish with short paste-covered strips, overlapping each adjoining strip. (See Illustration 9.) This will make a smooth edge for your dish.

Now bake the bowl in the oven at 250° again until it is completely dry. Keep your eye on the dish while it is baking. Don't let it get too brown. When it is dry, take your dish from the oven and examine it. Hit it with your knuckles; a well-made dish should give a hard sound—like a drum.

Sand the dish with fine emery paper until it is smooth. Coat it with raw linseed oil and bake it again. Decorate it and coat it with at least three coats of thinned black lacquer (sanding it between coats) and your nut dish will be complete.

Illus. 10.

With the self-confidence that comes from making your first papier mâché object, you are now ready to make a large papier mâché bowl. Use it for tossing and serving salads; large bowls like this are expensive to purchase.

Materials Checklist

stack of newspapers
heavy rubber balloon or
beach ball or
round-bottomed plastic dishpan or
large wooden salad bowl
flour and powdered resin glue mixture (see page 7)
raw linseed oil
black brushing lacquer

This project is made in exactly the same fashion as the preceding one, but is made larger—much larger. Even though your bowl or balloon or dishpan mould is a large one, you won't need to tear longer strips of newspaper. Use strips built up from quartered newspaper strips by pasting the four-thickness strips end to end on the mould with a one-inch overlap to make strips of the required length.

If you use a beach ball or balloon as the mould, set it in a large bucket and build your bowl over the exposed end of the ball or balloon. (See Illustration 11.) This makes it easier to hold.

Whatever you use, though, build up your bowl in exactly the same way as you made the nut dish, but make it thicker. One-half inch would not be too thick.

When your bowl is thick enough, remove it from the mould and bake it in the oven; you can allow it to dry naturally—in the sun, if possible.

Build up a rim with strips on the bottom of the bowl at least ½" higher than the mid-bottom to give a firm base to the bowl, so it will not rock.

Let the rim dry and brush the entire bowl with raw linseed oil. Bake at 250°. Sand and finish as described on pages 90 through 93.

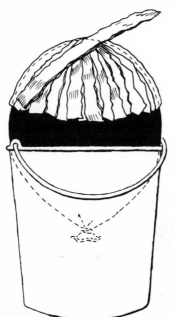

Illus. 11. *A bucket makes an ideal holder for a balloon or beach ball which is being used as a mould.*

Illus. 12.

Your large salad bowl will need a matching salad fork and serving spoon in papier mâché to be used for mixing salads and in serving from the bowl. To make these, you will use a slightly different technique. You may want to use an existing salad fork and spoon from which to copy. However, if the bowl that you have made is extra large, the fork and spoon will have to be in proportion. (A 2-foot diameter bowl, for example, would take an 18-inch long fork and spoon.)

Materials Checklist

    stack of newspapers
    flour and powdered resin glue mixture
    raw linseed oil
    black brushing lacquer

Cut a paper armature to the size and shape of the spoon and fork you

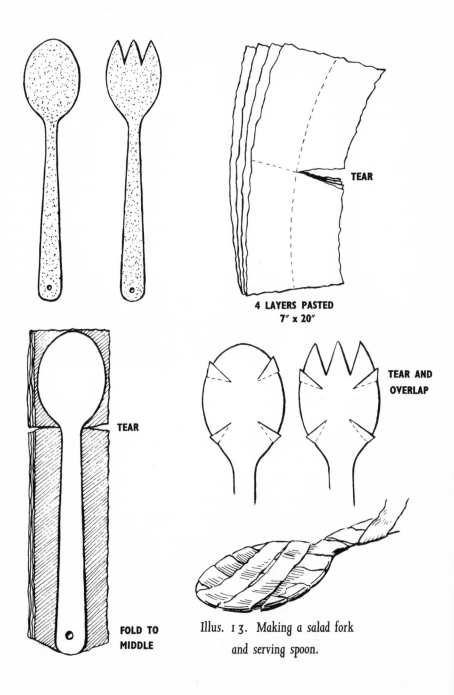

4 LAYERS PASTED
7″ x 20″

TEAR

TEAR AND OVERLAP

TEAR

FOLD TO MIDDLE

Illus. 13. *Making a salad fork and serving spoon.*

want to make. A paper armature takes and holds the curved shape of the fork and spoon very nicely. (See Illustration 13.)

Cover the armature on one side only with strips of paste-coated newspaper, as in the preceding projects. Criss-cross the layers of newspaper strips as you go—they should only be as long as needed for that layer, however. Press each layer firmly to remove air bubbles and excess water.

Now bake your fork and spoon in the oven. Cover the other side of the paper armature with paste-coated strips and bake again. When the objects are dry, trim the edges.

Add more strips of paste-coated paper to the fork and spoon until the desired thicknesses are achieved. Wrap the edges neatly, too, for a more finished effect. Sand the fork and spoon smooth and soak them with raw linseed oil. Bake again in a 250° oven. Finish them with black brushing lacquer.

Illus. 14. *The completed salad bowl and utensils. The papier mâché scoop is a useful adjunct to the kitchen.*

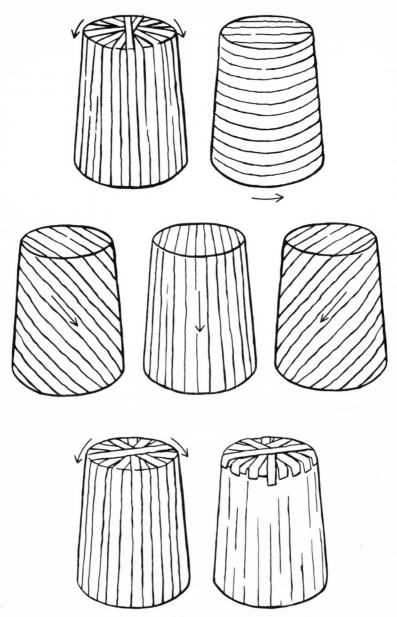

Illus. 15. Making the round wastepaper basket.

3. Putting Your Skills to Work

ROUND WASTEPAPER BASKET

No home ever has enough wastepaper baskets. Different rooms require different sizes and shapes. One as big as a 50-gallon oil drum will do nicely for a studio or workroom; a small basket for the boudoir; one beside a man's chest of drawers for the laundry cardboards from his shirts. Wastepaper baskets are convenient alongside writing desk, sewing table, bed, coffee table in the living room, and in the laundry.

Materials Checklist

stack of newspapers
flour and powdered resin glue mixture
wastepaper basket or pail (to serve as a mould)

Make the round wastepaper basket in the same way as the nut dish or the salad bowl. The extra strength needed in the bottom portion of the wastepaper basket is obtained by using extra layers of paste-coated paper strips. (See Illustration 15.) You will see this if you apply only about eight layers of strips and then turn the basket and mould right side up and take out the mould. The basket will sag like a child's socks wrinkling around the ankles. But a few extra layers across the bottom and about 6 inches up the sides will keep the wastepaper basket standing up straight until it is dry.

If you like the sagged look, leave it that way. Of course, the basket may be dried on the mould. But anything that will not stand up by itself when wet will be weak when dry. Bake in a 250° oven. Oil with raw linseed oil and bake again.

Decorate your finished wastepaper basket with an appropriate motif, after sanding it smooth. It can then be done in one of the finishes described on pages 90 through 93, depending on the effect that you want to achieve.

CYLINDRICAL LAMPSHADES

Illus. 16.

Lampshades are most often cylinders or truncated cones. If you wish to make a rectangular lampshade, see the instructions for making rectangular trays on page 27.

The lampshades in this project are simply upside-down wastepaper baskets without bottoms. Because a lampshade should transmit light, now you can experiment with various lovely sheer papers, wrapping tissue, rice papers—in clear, white and vivid hues.

Materials Checklist
thin paper such as tissue or rice paper
wallpaper paste
lampshade fixture
pail or bucket (to serve as a mould)

First buy or salvage from a discarded lampshade the metal wire frame that attaches the shade to the lamp. Fold the wet, paste-coated paper right around the wire frame and build this frame into the lampshade. Once this bond has been established, you may be as simple or as fanciful as you wish.

Wallpaper paste is used as the adhesive for making lampshades because of its ability to pass light. The flour and powdered resin glue mixture that you have been using would give you a dense and opaque lampshade.

You should experiment with applying the paper in various ways to achieve different effects. For example, on one shade you can make the paper pleated or shirred. (See Illustration 16.) Apply it in layers of different colors. Remember that a lampshade doesn't have to be as strong as a wastepaper basket.

Dry the lampshade on or off its mould. When it is thoroughly dry, test it. If it bends excessively or if there are weak places in it, build it up with added paper and paste and make it firm and stiff. But don't overdo it—the lampshade should pass light, so don't make it too thick.

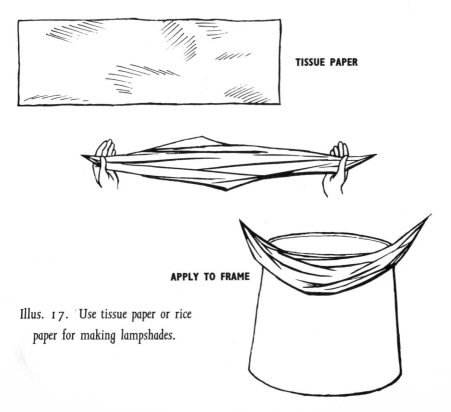

TISSUE PAPER

APPLY TO FRAME

Illus. 17. Use tissue paper or rice
paper for making lampshades.

ROUND TRAYS

Illus. 18.

Trays are merely variations on wastepaper baskets, lampshades and other cylindrical objects. The principles of construction are exactly the same—only the size and shape are different.

Materials Checklist

stack of newspapers
flour and powdered resin glue mixture
large iron skillet (to serve as a mould)
raw linseed oil

A large iron skillet makes an ideal mould. Make the bottom edges of the tray thicker than in previous projects; this is necessary for strength. A thickness of one-half inch is not excessive for a large tray bottom, gradually diminishing to one-quarter or three-eighths of an inch at the rim.

Place, right side up, the skillet and its papier mâché tray on a baking sheet —that is, as though you were going to cook something in the skillet. If your tray is too large, you will have to let it dry naturally on the skillet, but give it plenty of time. If your oven is large enough, bake it in the oven. Dry it with the weight of the skillet pressing down on the tray and the flat baking sheet. This will keep the tray from warping and will give the bottom the flatness it needs if you expect to carry dishes or glasses on it.

Sand the tray thoroughly with emery paper and decorate it with a gay design. (See Illustration 18.) Finish with one of the finishes described on pages 90 through 93.

Rectangular trays in various sizes have a thousand uses. They make wonderful desk caddies for holding paper clips and similar supplies that usually spill all over a desk drawer. They make excellent containers for jewels and other objects in a woman's dressing table. Or you can use them to store handkerchiefs, socks and other articles in a man's wardrobe.

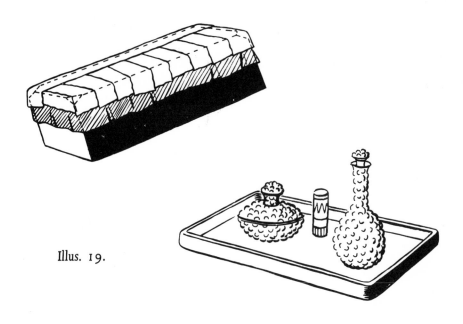

Illus. 19.

Materials Checklist

stack of newspapers
flour and powdered resin glue mixture
cardboard boxes (to serve as moulds)
raw linseed oil

Make rectangular trays in various sizes by using existing cardboard boxes as moulds. Removal of the finished trays from the moulds will be easier if you first cut off the corners of the boxes serving as moulds. Boxes measuring 6 to 8 inches on a side are just right for making trays; on a box this size, you should take off about a quarter of an inch at each corner.

Also to make it easier to remove the trays from their moulds, cover each side of the box with four layers of dry paper and then cover this with a layer of aluminium foil.

Apply about eight layers of paper strips to the box, pressing and smoothing each layer firmly. Bake this in the oven, allowing it to dry thoroughly on the mould. Remove from the mould. Check the tray for sturdiness, adding additional pieces of paper or paper strips where necessary. Trim the edges cleanly with a sharp knife. If the edges of the tray appear thin after trimming them, build them up with additional strips and bake again in the oven.

Sand the tray smooth with emery paper. Decorate and finish as described on pages 90 through 93.

RECTANGULAR TRAYS WITH DIVIDERS

Even more suitable for sorting desk articles or keeping jewels separated are trays with dividers.

Materials Checklist

stack of newspapers
flour and powdered resin glue mixture
boxes (to serve as moulds)
pieces of thin cardboard (to make dividers)
raw linseed oil

Make these trays exactly as you made the preceding trays. Cut out strips of thin cardboard for dividers, and then paste them in place after the trays have been dried and removed from the moulds. Fasten the dividers by means of strips of paper pasted at the joints. Add layers until the desired thickness is reached.

Smooth with emery paper. Finish as described in the chapter on finishes.

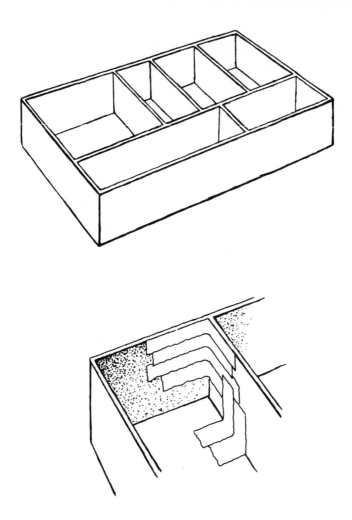

Illus. 20. Making rectangular trays with dividers.

SECTIONAL SHELVES

Illus. 21. Sectional shelves of papier mâché have a thousand uses.

These sectional shelves make ideal additions to the kitchen or workshop. They can be made up of a number of regular-sized boxes, or they can be built up from various odd-sized boxes. The latter makes a more interesting and sometimes more useful arrangement, for it will accommodate various-sized tools and utensils.

Materials Checklist

stack of newspapers
flour and powdered resin glue mixture
cardboard boxes (these can range in size from pill boxes to shoe boxes)
large sheet of plywood
1 x 2 inch waste lumber
raw linseed oil

To begin, nail 1 x 2 inch strips all around the edge of the plywood sheet to the size you want your finished shelf to be. These strips will serve to hold the shelf in place on the plywood while it is drying—to ensure good adhesion between the sections. Such a frame will enable you to make additional sectional-shelf units that can be fitted together.

Now place your collection of boxes within the strips in the order in which you want them. You may have to cut some boxes down to a different size in order to fit them in. They must fit tightly and completely. (See Illustration 22.)

Taking out one box at a time, coat each side of the box (but not the bottom) and replace it so that it becomes fastened to the next one. Be careful that the whole assemblage *does not* get glued to the plywood sheet; use glue sparingly.

Now cover the inside bottom of each box with a layer of paste-coated strips of newspaper. Cover the sides of the boxes in the same fashion. Overlap each row of strips over the next row slightly so as to have continuous coverage.

Criss-cross additional strips in other directions until the boxes have been covered with about eight layers of paste-coated paper strips.

Place the entire assemblage in a warm dry place and allow to dry. When it is thoroughly dry, the unit may be lifted off the plywood.

Turn the sectional shelves over so that the back is upwards. Now add paste-coated strips to the back until about eight layers have been built up. Allow to dry thoroughly again.

Sand smooth with emery paper and finish according to the instructions on finishes on pages 90 through 93.

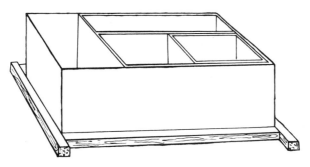

Illus. 22. Build sectional shelves in a wooden frame.

HAT BOXES

Illus. 23.

Hat boxes are always useful for summer or winter storage of hats and other articles, and they make wonderful gifts. You will need a round or an oval hat box to serve as a mould.

Materials Checklist

    stack of newspapers
    flour and powdered resin glue mixture
    round or oval hat box
    raw linseed oil

Build the hat box by the strip method, using an existing hat box as a mould.

Bake and surface as in previous projects.

In order to ensure a correct-fitting lid, use the bottom of the hat box in the following way:

Cover the bottom of the box with aluminium foil. Build up a shallow lid by the strip method on the bottom of the hat box. (See Illustration 24.) Let this dry naturally until it is partially stiff, then remove the lid from the bottom of the box.

Now cover the top edge of the box with aluminium foil. Place the partially dry lid in position on top of the hat box. Coat box and lid with raw linseed oil. Complete the drying by baking in the oven until thoroughly dry.

This hat box is best decorated with torn squares of colored paper using the collage method described on page 88.

Many boxes that are intended only to last long enough for the trip from a shop to your home can have their lives extended if you will use them as armatures (instead of as moulds) and build papier mâché right on to them. Besides hat boxes, you can use shoe boxes, blanket boxes, and similar boxes constructed of relatively flimsy cardboard. Apply strips of paste-coated paper directly to the boxes inside and out.

Finish such boxes in exactly the same manner as boxes made on a mould. However, because of the stiffening qualities of the strip-covered armature, you may omit the linseed oil application.

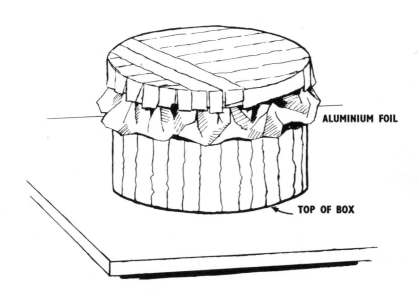

Illus. 24. Making the lid of the papier mâché hat box.

4. Folded and Rolled Objects

Now that you have mastered the method of making things from paste-coated paper strips in the flat state, you may want to attempt objects utilizing a new technique—folding and rolling the pieces of newspaper. There is nothing complicated about it, and it will allow you to make some new and unusual shapes.

BEADS

Here is a method for making small beads for necklaces; when finished, the beads will be one half-inch in size or less. They can be smaller or even as large as an egg—depending on the size of the pieces of paper you start with. Beaded curtains are again popular, and an unusual beaded curtain can be made with large papier mâché beads. The beads are so light that they will almost caress you as you go through a door.

Materials Checklist

stack of newspapers
flour and powdered resin glue mixture
thread
No. OO crochet hook (a heavy piece of wire from a wire coat hanger may be substituted)
clear lacquer and lacquer thinner

Tear quarter sheets of paste-coated newspaper into four strips. Combine them and tear each four-layered strip in half.

Using one half of each of these strips at a time, fold it on itself (like rolling) so that you have a strip measuring about one-half inch across and 5 inches long.

Illus. 25.

Press this with your fingers from the middle outwards to flatten it and to remove excess water, paste and air.

Remove about three-quarters of the thickness of each end of these strips so that the ends are not as thick as the rest of the strip. This thinning of the material at the ends makes it easier to blend the ends in when you make the beads. (See Illustration 25.)

Using a No. OO crochet hook, wrap the strip around the shank, holding the strip firmly on the crochet hook as you wrap it round. Smooth it firmly with the fingers and blend the end of the strip in smoothly.

Slip the bead off the hook and smooth it lightly with your fingers. Be careful not to change its shape or to close the hole while it is soft.

Make as many beads as you want for a necklace. You should be able to make enough for a 3-foot string in less than half an hour.

Bake your beads in the oven on a baking sheet or a sheet of heavy aluminium foil. When dry, they may be sanded lightly with emery paper and finished in the following manner.

Buy small cans of clear lacquer and lacquer thinner. (For small numbers of beads, you can use clear nail polish, and use polish remover in place of the lacquer thinner.)

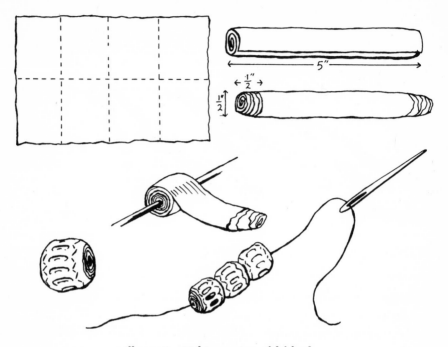

Illus. 26. *Making papier mâché beads.*

Place a small amount (say, one-half cup) of clear lacquer in a paper cup. Add an equal quantity of lacquer thinner.

String your papier mâché beads loosely on a thin thread and dip them in the lacquer mixture. Lift out and let dry. (Lacquer dries rapidly.) Dip the beads twice a day until five coats have been applied. Use thinned lacquer for the first two coats; after that, use the lacquer full strength. Remember that lacquer is highly inflammable and do your bead-dipping away from a fire or flame. Out-of-doors is best.

String your finished beads on bead-stringing thread. (You can use dental floss as a substitute.) For beaded curtains, raffia makes an exciting contrast of texture with the roughly shaped beads. Knot the raffia between each bead to hold the beads in place. Alternate large and small beads for variety, too.

Beautiful buttons, especially large ones, can be expensive. Here is a way of making smart-looking buttons with an individual style.

Materials Checklist

stack of newspapers
flour and powdered resin glue mixture
{ button shanks or
{ 6-inch square of plywood and 2 or 4 one-inch nails

There are two ways to make buttons: One is to use a shank in each button; the other kind has two or four holes through each button for sewing the button to the fabric.

For buttons with a shank, get one or two dozen shanks from a dressmaker or from a dressmakers' supplier. These will be more than you need, so make some extra buttons as gifts. Shape the buttons, making them flat, rounded or sculpted as flowers, insects, animals or random non-representational shapes. Bake them and sand them.

Finish them with one of the finishes described on pages 90 through 93. Cement the papier mâché button to the shank with some casein glue.

Buttons with holes for sewing are made in a different way:

Nail two or four nails through a 6-inch square of plywood. Make the nails about one-quarter inch apart.

Build each button around the nails, using strips or bits of paste-coated newspaper. (See Illustration 27.) If the buttons are all to be more or less the same shape, draw this shape directly on the plywood. If it is circular, inscribe it with a compass. When the button has been built up to the shape and thickness that you want, slide it off the nail and make another.

Bake your buttons on a baking sheet or on a sheet of heavy aluminium foil. Sand, decorate and finish.

The texture of papier mâché buttons is particularly suitable for use with woollens and heavy cotton materials. They look just right on knitted dresses, sweaters, coats and most casual or sports clothes. Dainty, tiny buttons can also be made from papier mâché for the sheerest chiffon evening gown or négligée. They are so delicate and light that they will not weigh down the sheerest fabric. Similarly, even the largest papier mâché buttons will still be feather-light and will not change the line of the garment on which they are used.

Illus. 27. *Two ways of making papier mâché buttons.*

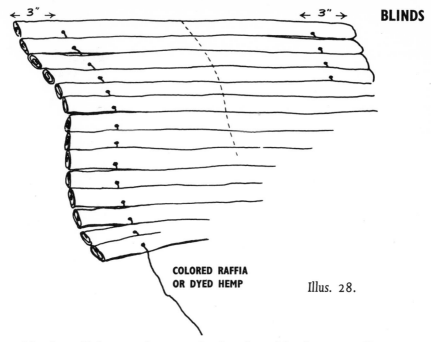

← 3" →   ← 3" →

**COLORED RAFFIA
OR DYED HEMP**   Illus. 28.

These blinds will be similar to split bamboo blinds, yet will retain a texture peculiar to papier mâché. You and everyone will be charmed by the individuality of the papier mâché blinds you make.

Materials Checklist

stack of newspapers
flour and powdered resin glue mixture

First measure the window for which the blinds are intended. The blinds can either fit inside the window or lap over the frame by about 2 inches.

Start with a thick (about 32-page) section of newspaper. Open this at the middle and tear at the fold. Tear each sheet in half again lengthwise. Make a stack of these half sheets, which will measure about 7 by 22 inches.

Dip sheets in water to wet them. Remove the sheets and apply paste with your hand. Smooth off excess paste.

Fold this sheet in half lengthwise. Apply more paste, remove excess and fold again. Keep folding in half, pressing and smoothing until you have a strip about an inch wide. Your blinds will be even more attractive if you vary the width of the strips—these can be from one-half inch to 1½ inches in width.

Make enough strips for the length of your window.

Smooth each strip lightly with emery paper. Tint the slats for the blinds with dye and finish with several thin coats of clear lacquer.

Using two pieces of colored raffia or dyed hemp, lace up the blinds as shown in Illustration 28. The end lacing should be about 3 inches from each end. An extra lacing of raffia or hemp in the middle of long blinds will keep them more even.

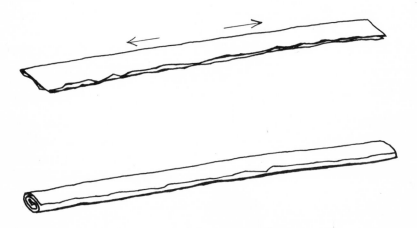

Illus. 29. Making papier mâché blinds.

Illus. 30.

Woven baskets look easy to make, but are tricky in the larger sizes unless you know the technique. Practise by making some smaller woven baskets before attempting larger ones. The mould cannot be removed from the basket until it is completely dry.

Materials Checklist

stack of newspapers
flour and powdered resin glue mixture
wastepaper basket or bucket (to serve as a mould)

First turn the mould upside down and measure the distance from one rim up one side, across the bottom, and down the opposite side to the rim. This distance determines the length of the longest strips you will need.

Make the strips in exactly the same way as the strips described in the preceding project for the making of blinds. For smaller baskets, make the strips narrow, about one-half inch wide. Strips one inch or more in width are appropriate in larger baskets. Strive for variety rather than uniformity in the width of your strips; it will make your finished woven wastepaper basket more interesting.

Lay strips across the mould in a parallel pattern. Tear one strip in half and insert one of the halves among the other strips, pasting it at the middle. (See Illustration 31.) There must be an odd number of splines (uprights) in your basket, otherwise you will not be able to weave the sides.

Start your weaving of strips from the inside at the middle. Splice ends of strips together to give a continuous effect; be sure that each strip ends inside the basket before splicing—you may have to tear off a piece at the end of the strip to achieve this.

Dry the woven basket on the mould until it is absolutely dry. Don't remove the basket from the mould while it is still wet or it will collapse in a heap. After it has dried, take your basket from the mould and check for sturdiness. Pay particular attention to the adhesion between vertical and horizontal strips where they cross. If there is poor adhesion between any crossing strips, apply some of the paste mixture to the joint and squeeze it tightly together. (A weight on the joint will help to hold it while it is drying.) Allow the basket to dry and check it again. Repeat the reinforcing until the basket is sturdy. Apply linseed oil all over the basket, inside and out, and let the basket dry. Finish the woven basket with several coats of thinned clear lacquer.

Other possibilities for woven articles using this method are summer woven-basketry handbags, hats, fruit baskets or even a woven basket for storing kindling wood by the fireplace.

Illus. 31. Detail of the weaving of the woven wastepaper basket.

CHERUBS AND FIGURINES

Illus. 32.

Cherubs and similar figurines are made over a wire armature, as anything that has appendages should be.

Materials Checklist

two light wire coat hangers
stack of newspapers
flour and powdered resin glue mixture
colored brushing lacquers

A child is four heads tall. Make a rough sketch on paper to the size you want your figures to be and then make a wire skeleton or armature to fit. Hang this from the ceiling (or a shelf) by a strong string while you are making the figure. (See Illustration 33.)

Pleat, twist and wrap sheets of paste-covered paper in successive layers on the armature. Bake the figure between each layer.

Fasten a small wire loop to the armature between the wings and attach a length of clear nylon thread to hang them. Two or more will swing and turn in a breeze; they will seem to be talking to one another.

One of the cherubs in Illustration 32 has been lacquered a brilliant orange; another is mahogany; the third is black.

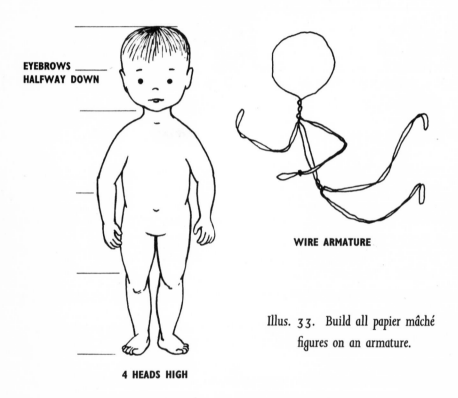

EYEBROWS
HALFWAY DOWN

WIRE ARMATURE

4 HEADS HIGH

Illus. 33. Build all papier mâché figures on an armature.

5. The Art of Working with Mash

There is still another "material" into which newspapers can be converted. It is called "mash." It opens up a whole new world, because it is so different in texture and composition from the laminated strips of newspaper.

HOW TO MAKE MASH

One of the advantages of working with mash is the fact that it can be made in advance and kept. Mash improves in texture and consistency with aging.

Materials Checklist

2 large galvanized or enamel buckets

stack of newspapers

flour (no resin glue is used)

oil of wintergreen

2 asbestos stove mats

strainer or collander

whisk (see page 94)

Tear newspapers into quarter sheets. Tear narrow strips of newspaper one-quarter to one-half inch wide with the grain of the paper. Bunch these together in your hand.

Next tear the strips crosswise into pieces about one to 1½ inches long. Fill one of your buckets with the dry, torn pieces of newspaper. Fill the other bucket with water and bring it to a boil.

Into the boiling water sprinkle the pieces of newspaper as if you were cooking noodles. Stir the pieces of paper to separate them well.

Cook the paper until the fibres are broken down and the paper has disintegrated. Add water from time to time if necessary to keep the bucket full.

Add one-half teaspoon of oil of wintergreen. This keeps the mash smelling sweet and prevents the growth of moulds and fungi.

Using the whisk you have made (see page 94) or an electric beater, if you have one, beat until the mixture is smooth. Any small pieces that happen to escape the beating process may be left in the mash, except when it is to be used in fine casting—in which case the pieces can be taken out as they are found.

Drain in the wire strainer or collander until there is no water standing in the mixture. The mash will be moist and will still contain much water.

Measure four measuring cups of flour and add these to each gallon of mash that you have made. Mix well.

Now place the bucket back on the stove with an asbestos mat under the bucket. Cook at the lowest heat. Remember that flour scorches easily. Cover the bucket for the first hour until the mash has heated throughout. Remove the cover from the bucket and continue cooking (adding no water) until the mash is stiff enough to stand in piles by itself.

Dump the mash out upon about a dozen thicknesses of newspaper to cool. The mash may be used as soon as it is cool enough to handle or it may be stored in the refrigerator. In hot weather, cool mash is pleasant to work with. In the winter, it is probably a good idea to let it reach room temperature before trying to work with it.

You may ask, "Why do I need the two buckets? Wouldn't one be enough?" Of course, the answer is that one would do very nicely, and there's nothing magical or special about the number two. It's just that one batch of paper may be cooking in the first bucket while the other is cooling. If you find yourself using large quantities of mash, you may find yourself wishing for several of those old-fashioned huge copper kettles that were once a part of every washday scene.

In the projects that follow, you will create new and different articles of papier mâché by adding mash to articles made by the strip method or to folded paper or wire armatures. Conversely, mash can be added to any of the earlier projects; it goes on as easily as modelling clay. You will be surprised at the difference even a thin layer of mash can make in a papier mâché article. Because of its very nature, mash also opens up new opportunities for decorating your papier mâché articles with designs incised into the mash. (See pages 88 and 89 for a description of this method.)

Illus. 34. These candle holders and candles will add a festive touch to any table.

Illus. 35. Papier mâché children's building blocks are simple and easy to make.

ROUND BOWL

Illus. 36.

You make a simple armature for this bowl from one piece of four-thickness newspaper by cutting or tearing it. No mould is used. Cover it with mash inside and out and your bowl is finished. It will look crude and it is crude, but its primitiveness only adds charm to the piece.

Materials Checklist

stack of newspapers
flour and powdered resin glue mixture
mash

Paste four quarter-sheets of newspaper together. Cut or tear them while still wet to the circular shape shown in Illustration 37. Next cut or tear about six slits into the circumference of the circle, as shown in Illustration 38.

Overlap the cut or torn edges of the slits to form a bowl shape. Bake this in the oven until dry and trim the top edge with scissors.

Line the inside of this bowl-armature with mash. Bake again. Turn it upside down and cover the outside of the bowl with another layer of mash. Bake once more. Sand and touch up the edges and any thin spots with a dab of mash. Let dry and finish.

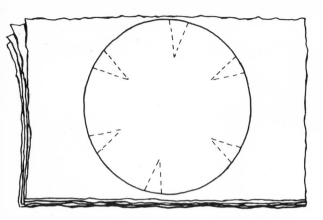

Illus. 37. Paste four quarter newspaper sheets together and tear to circular shape.

Illus. 38. Cut or tear slits in the circle.

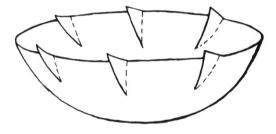

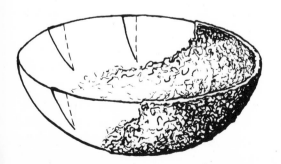

Illus. 39. Line the inside of the bowl with mash.

49

FLOWER POT COVERS

Illus. 40.

The French word to describe these objects is "cache-pot," which translates roughly as "pot hiders." These are not easy to find in shops, so they are particularly good things to make as gifts.

Materials Checklist

    stack of newspapers
    flour and powdered resin glue mixture
    mash

If you were to use a flower pot of the same size as the one you want to cover as a mould, you would find that your flower pot cover was too tight. The solution to this problem is to use as a mould a flower pot of the next larger size.

Flower pot covers are made in the same way as wastepaper baskets—except that they have no bottoms. In other words, they are merely sleeves to cover ordinary clay or plastic flower pots.

Build an armature of four pasted layers of paper and bake in the oven. Next cover the inside with a one-quarter inch layer of mash and bake again. Cover the outside, too, with a one-quarter inch layer of mash and bake once more. (See Illustration 40.)

Turn out napkin rings in a papier mâché assembly line, and you will have plenty of these popular and useful objects to give away as gifts.

Materials Checklist

stack of newspapers

flour and powdered resin glue mixture

mash

Make these little rings about 2½ inches across. First make rings of folded paper strips (as in the papier mâché blinds and the woven wastepaper baskets). Bake these armature rings in the oven until dry and cover them with mash, both inside and out.

Twelve dozen could easily be made in a day. They are excellent for experimenting with decorating, coloring and finishing techniques. (See Illustration 41.)

Illus. 41. You will never want for napkin rings if you make them of papier mâché.

CLEANSING TISSUE BOX COVER

Cover the unpretty box that cleansing tissues often come in and you can place cleansing tissues throughout the house. They will never seem out of place in an attractively covered dispenser.

Materials Checklist

stack of newspapers
flour and powdered resin glue mixture
cleansing tissue box (to serve as a mould)
mash

First you should select a box of the type that you intend to cover. The opening through which the tissues are dispensed may vary.

Build up the size of the box with about a half-inch thickness of newspaper and then cover it with aluminium foil. Be sure to leave the opening of the box "open."

Now cover the mould with a one-quarter inch coating of papier mâché. Bake this in the oven until it is dry.

When it is dry, cover the inside of your papier mâché box with a very thin ($\frac{1}{8}$ inch) coating of mash.

CHILD'S STOOL AND TOY BOX

Here is an object that is simply and quickly made, yet will serve several purposes.

Materials Checklist

heavy cardboard carton at least
12 inches square

mash

Illus. 43. *This useful addition to a child's room looks like an oversized children's building block.*

Cover the cardboard carton with about half a dozen layers of dry newspaper. Applying the mash liberally, coat the mould to a thickness of about ¾ of an inch all around. If your mould is not too large, bake the stool and toy box in the oven while it is still on its mould. Otherwise, let it dry naturally—this may take a week or more.

Remove from the mould when dry and coat the inside with a one-quarter inch thick layer of mash. Build up the corners thicker on the inside to reinforce the box. Remember that in a child's room it is likely to receive some rough treatment.

Color each side a separate shade by dyeing (see page 89) and paint a large (8-inch) letter of the alphabet on each of the five sides. If you make several of these combination stools and toy boxes, children will love to use them as giant building blocks.

This makes an excellent project for finishing with epoxy coatings. (See page 93.)

Illus. 44.

RECTANGULAR BOXES WITH LIDS AND LIPS

Here is a simple method for making boxes with lids that match.

Materials Checklist

stack of newspapers
flour and powdered resin glue mixture
mash

With a pencil, draw tearing-and-folding lines on one quarter-sheet of newspaper. (See Illustration 45.) Now paste four quarter-sheets of newspaper together, making the marked sheet the top one.

Cut the paper with a pair of scissors along the cutting lines. Now fold into a deep tray shape, as shown in Illustration 46. Bake this in a 250° oven and trim the top edge with scissors so that it is even.

Cover the top with paste-coated strips; build these up to a thickness of four layers. Bake again. Smooth off any rough edges.

Cover the top and outside of the box with a $\frac{1}{8}$ inch thick layer of mash. While this is still relatively soft, cut a line at the midpoint around the sides into the mash layer with the back of a knife blade. This line will be used as a guide line for cutting later. (See Illustration 47.)

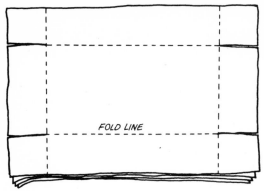

CUT LINE

FOLD LINE

Illus. 45. Draw tearing-and-folding lines like this.

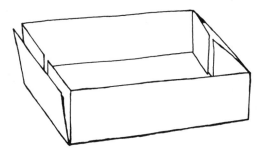

Illus. 46. Fold into a deep tray shape.

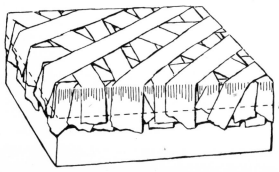

Illus. 47. Mark a line in the mash with the back of a knife blade.

CUT LINE

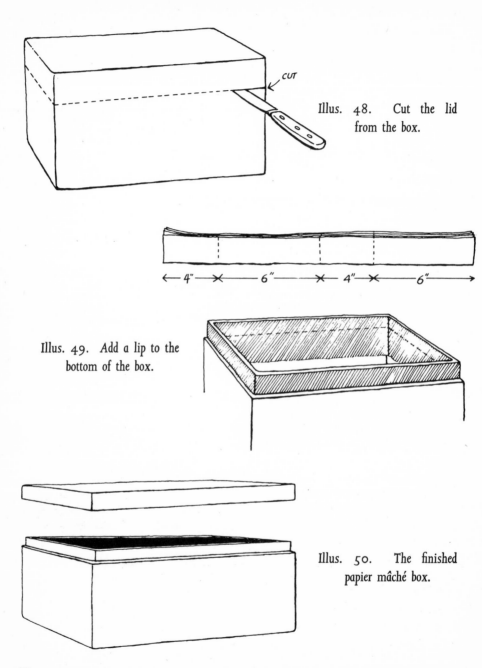

Illus. 48. Cut the lid from the box.

Illus. 49. Add a lip to the bottom of the box.

Illus. 50. The finished papier mâché box.

Bake the box in the oven until the mash is dry.

Cut the lid from the box with a sharp knife, following the guide line incised in the mash. (See Illustration 48.)

Now add four thicknesses of 2½ inch wide paper to the inside of the box to form the lip. (See Illustration 49.) Bake the box once again.

Line the inside of the box with a ⅛ inch layer of mash. Place the lid on the box and bake again. (Baking with the lid on makes it less likely that the lid will warp out of shape.)

If the box is to have a surface decoration, add more mash to the outside and make designs in the mash while it is still soft. Bake again and your box is finished. If you prefer a plainer box, leave it as it comes from the oven and finish according to the directions on pages 90 through 93.

Illus. 51. Trinket boxes of papier mâché. The making of incised designs is described on pages 88 and 89.

PENCIL CUPS

These forms represent the ultimate in the combination of the techniques of strip-pasting and the use of mash. The pencil cups shown in Illustration 52 were made this way:

Materials Checklist

    stack of newspapers
    flour and powdered resin glue mixture
    mash

Paste four one-quarter sheets of newspaper together. Tear these in fourths, so that the resulting pieces measure about 3 by 4 inches. Overlap the edges so that you make a cylinder. (See Illustration 53.)

Bake these in the oven until dry—but do not let them turn brown—standing them on end on a baking sheet or a large piece of half-inch screening.

Remove from the oven and trim the top and bottom edges of each cylinder with scissors. Cover the inside of the cylinders with a layer of mash ⅛ inch thick. Bake again.

Illus. 52.

Illus. 53. Make a cylinder of four pasted quarter sheets of newspaper.

CONCAVE BOTTOM

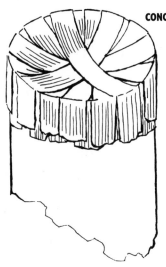

Illus. 54. Cover one end of the cylinder with strips in a star pattern.

Cover one end with strips of paste-coated newspaper in a star pattern. (This "bottom" should be slightly concave to give a firm base to your pencil cup. See Illustration 54.) These should overlap on the sides of the cylinder by at least one inch.

Bake again. Now cover the inside bottom with mash and bake once more. Cover the outside of the cylinders with mash one-quarter inch thick.

Illus. 55.

SPICE AND CONDIMENT CANISTERS

No one seems to have enough attractive spice and condiment canisters to hold the collection a good cook uses.

Materials Checklist

stack of newspapers
flour and powdered resin glue mixture
corks, $1\frac{1}{2}$ inches wide
mash

Make enough cylinders 3, 4, and 5 inches tall to make a full set. (See the preceding project.)

Their diameters should be 2, $2\frac{1}{2}$, and 3 inches, respectively.

Cover bottom with a star-shaped pattern of paste-coated strips, indenting them one-half inch to make a concave surface. (See Illustration 56.)

Bake.

Cover the inside with a $\frac{1}{8}$ inch layer of mash.

Bake and sand thoroughly.

Make a star-shaped top of thin paste-coated strips stretched straight across to make a flat surface.

Bake.

Add a layer of mash one-half inch thick to the outside top. Make a hole by turning and pressing a wet cork into the middle-top of the canister

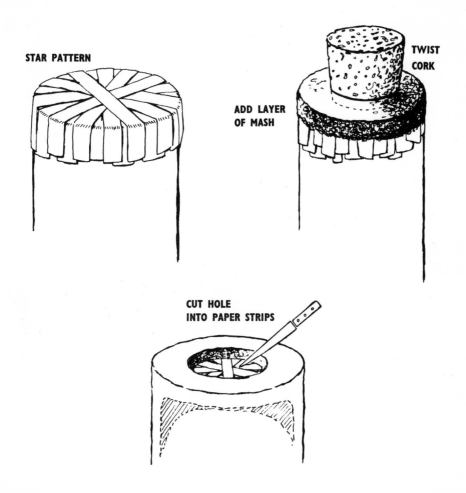

STAR PATTERN

ADD LAYER
OF MASH

TWIST
CORK

CUT HOLE
INTO PAPER STRIPS

Illus. 56. These additional steps will turn pencil cups into spice and condiment canisters.

down to the paper-strip top. To make the cork the right size for the finished hole, cut the cork in half and use the top half.

Cover the sides of the canister with a one-quarter inch thick layer of mash and bake only until dry, not brown.

Cut around the cork hole with a sharp knife to remove the paper strips that served as an armature.

Using your index finger, add mash around the inside of the top where it joins the sides. Cover paper armature strips on the underside of the top smoothly.

Bake to a toast-brown color.

Smooth inside and out with emery paper.

Dip in a clear finish. Give several coats, letter the names of the spices and condiments, add the cork, and you are done.

Illus. 57. Four dozen different spice and condiment canisters will open the door to culinary delights.

Illus. 58.

These shakers are labelled flour, salt, and powdered sugar, and are designed to be used near the stove.

Materials Checklist

stack of newspapers
flour and powdered resin glue mixture
corks, 1½ inches wide
nail
mash

Paste four quarter-sheets of newspaper together. Make a cylinder about 3 inches in diameter.
Bake.

Add strips to one end in star pattern, indenting them about $\frac{3}{4}$ of an inch to make a concave bottom. Bake.

Cover the concave surface with a one-half inch layer of mash, making a hole by turning a wet cork in the mash. Cut a cork in half and use the top half to ensure the finished hole being the right size.

Bake only until dry.

Cover the inside of the cylinder with a $\frac{1}{8}$ inch layer of mash, reinforcing the inside top.

Bake only until dry.

Sand thoroughly.

Place strips of paper, pulled straight and flat, across the other end.

Bake only until dry.

Add a one-half inch layer of mash over the flat top. Punch 16 holes in the mash surface, using the nail and going down just to the paper armature. (See Illustration 59.) Bake.

Punch the holes on through the paper.

Sand and finish with bright dyes and several finish coats.

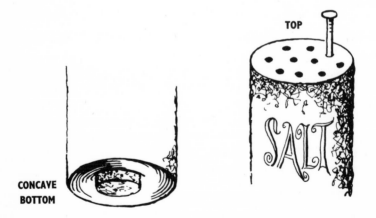

Illus. 59. Shakers are similar to canisters, but the cork is in the bottom.

Illus. 60.

The funnels (Illustration 60) were made to fill the spice canisters and shakers.

Materials Checklist

stack of newspapers
flour and powdered resin glue mixture

Paste four one-quarter sheets together.

Tear a piece of this laminated sheet 2 inches wide and 4 inches long. Make a tube from this piece about one inch in diameter and 2 inches long.

Cut a dry paper pattern for the upper part of the funnel. Do this by cutting a circle 8 inches in diameter. Cut a circle 2 inches in diameter from the middle. Half of this circle is your pattern.

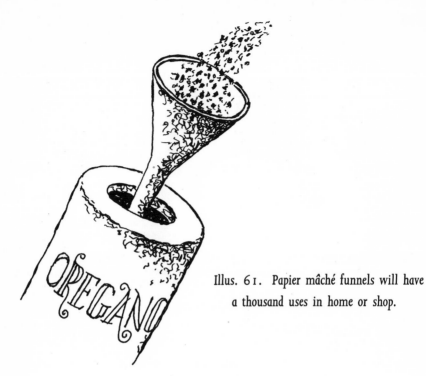

Illus. 61. *Papier mâché funnels will have
a thousand uses in home or shop.*

Tear an equivalent-sized half circle from the four thicknesses of pasted sheets.

Curve the half circle around the tube and fasten with three pasted strips.
Bake.

Tear a strip from a four-thickness sheet, one-half inch wide and 6 inches long. Place one inch of the strip on the inside of the cone. Curve it out to shape the handle, making sure you leave a hole at least one inch in diameter.
Bake.

Cover inside with about a $\frac{1}{8}$ inch thickness of mash.
Bake.

Cover outside with $\frac{1}{8}$ to one-quarter inch thickness of mash.
Bake.

Sand and fill.

Decorate and finish to match your kitchen.

PANELS

Illus. 62.

Decorative and architectural panels are an effective way to decorate a wall or even a whole room. Make designs in the panels you create, and you will have a truly unusual covering material. Papier mâché for architectural purposes is not such a novel idea—in 1834 the ceiling of the House of Lords in London was decorated in papier mâché and it is still in excellent condition.

Materials Checklist

    large sheet of plywood
    1 x 2 inch strips (for framing)
    mash

Cut out a piece of plywood slightly larger than the size of the finished panel you will make. Nail 1 x 2 inch framing strips all round. The papier mâché panel will be built up in this "mould."

Oil the inside of the mould thoroughly with raw linseed oil. Cover the inside bottom of the mould with about a half-dozen sheets of newspaper.

Lay a quarter-inch layer of mash in the mould. Let this dry. (Note: As you will soon discover, it is easier and quicker to dry papier mâché panels by building up several thin layers of mash than by attempting to dry one thick layer.)

For a screen divider, make your panel large and make two holes with a pencil at the upper end of the panel while the mash is setting. Decorate the panel in low relief or by incising designs in the surface. Suspend it from the ceiling by means of colored cords after finishing it as described in pages 90 through 93.

TOOLBOX

Illus. 63. Sturdy and strong, this tool box was made by covering a rough, splintery wooden packing box with mash. It was dried in the oven with door open. (The door could not be closed because the box was too large.) It has been left natural—no dye has been applied. For a more decorative than utilitarian box, the surface could be incised as described on pages 88 and 89 and then dyed or finished as described on pages 90 through 93.

LAMPSHADES

Illus. 64. These unusual lampshades were made with mash on a balloon mould. The upper shade is yellow, inside and out; the lower shade is a terra cotta color.

Illus. 65.

This case can be made to cover an unbeautiful alarm clock, case and all. Kitchen wall clocks are often functional, without being pretty. There is no law saying anything can't be beautiful or even just interesting as well as functional. (See Illustration 65.)

Materials Checklist

cardboard box
mash

Select a cardboard box for an armature, and cut a hole for the clock face. Cover the outside of the box with mash. Punch a border round the clock face and along all the corner edges. Bake.

Cover the inside of the box with mash, and bake.

Lay the case face down on the table and fit the face of the clock into the hole in the case. If your clock needs a shelf to hold it exactly in position (because the clock may be smaller than the case), build a shelf with strips of paste-coated paper, bake, cover with mash and bake again.

Puppet heads can be built in minutes, right in your hand, without all the extra processes of moulds. (See Illustration 66.)

Illus. 66.

Materials Checklist

stack of newspapers
flour and powdered resin glue mixture
mash

Make a little cylinder for the index finger, the thumb, and the little finger. Make them quite loose, about 2½ inches long.

Make two tubes of rolled newspaper, too, on which to build the feet.

Bake.

Crumple some dry paper in your hand to make about a 2 inch ball round one end of the index finger tube. Fasten it down with paper strips.

Bake.

Add one-quarter inch of mash as necessary to mould the shape of the head. Do the back of the head and the neck. Make a small ridge on the neck to give a place to secure the costume. Bake.

Build up the face and ears and bake again.

Build the hands and feet on the ends of the tubes with an armature of paste-coated paper strips. Bake.

Cover with mash and model to shape.

Bake all the pieces to a light golden brown (as near as possible to the shade of the skin of the character you are doing).

CANDLESTICKS

Illus. 67.

Illus. 68.

Candlelight has come to mean romance and festivity. These instructions can be adapted to any size candlestick. They are dimensioned for one small enough to bake in the oven.

Materials Checklist

stack of newspapers
flour and powdered resin glue mixture
lead weight
metal disc, cut from the top of a tin can, 2 inches in diameter
nail (2 inch finishing nail)
mash

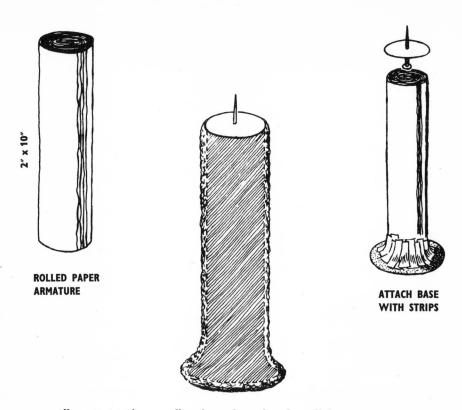

**ROLLED PAPER
ARMATURE**

2" x 10"

**ATTACH BASE
WITH STRIPS**

Illus. 69. Making candlesticks with mash and a rolled paper armature.

From paste-coated newspaper make a rolled-paper armature 2 inches by 10 inches. Bake.

Drive a nail through the middle of the 2 inch metal disc.

Cover one end of the 10 inch armature with mash.

Place the metal disc on top with the nail head down. Drive the nail part way in by hitting the nail on its point. (See Illustration 69.) Bake.

Make a 5 inch disc of four thicknesses of pasted paper. Bake.

Fasten circle to bottom of candlestick with pasted strips.

Bake, standing candlestick erect.

Cover with mash (a layer $\frac{3}{8}$ inch or more thick).

Punch a pattern of your selection on the surface. Bake.

Illus. 70.

Thanks to the interesting textures of papier mâché, here is a unique chess table and chessmen that will make you, the proud owner, the envy of your friends.

Materials Checklist

stack of newspapers
flour and powdered resin glue mixture
38 inch circle of ¼ inch plywood
32 small lead weights
mash (approximately 1 gallon needed)

Chess Table

For the table, cover the surface of the circle of plywood with a ⅜ inch layer of mash. Mark off the squares, 8 each way, 2¾ inches for each square. Set the plywood up at an angle so it will be easier to see and work on.

Punch the surface, almost to the wood, in a pattern in each square. The alternate squares that are to be black make one pattern, the squares to be

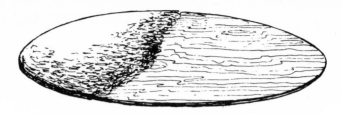

**PLYWOOD
TABLE TOP**

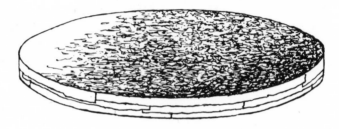

**ADD PASTED
PAPER EDGE**

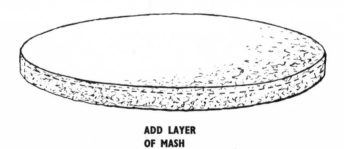

**ADD LAYER
OF MASH**

Illus. 71. Making the chess table top.

red, another. A border around the edge with flowers and leaves to fill in the curved space completes the pattern.

In working on such a large piece, the punching must be finished before the mash gets so dry as to form a skin on the top. If it begins to form, blot it with tapping motions with a damp cloth. This will only be a difficulty on dry, hot days. Ordinarily you will have several hours—much more than the few it will take you to punch-decorate the surface.

When the table top is thoroughly dry, paste a four-layer thickness of paste-coated paper around the edge, its top edge $\frac{1}{16}$ inch below the level of the top of the mash-covered top.

Let the edge dry with the table standing on its edge, leaning against the wall.

Cover the surface of the edge of the table with a $\frac{3}{4}$ inch thickness of mash and punch in a decorative border. Let dry. Sand.

Use water-color or dye to color the alternate squares red and black, the border and edge black.

Make a pedestal-shaped base of one-half inch screening, covered inside and out with a one-half inch layer of mash. Six screws attach it to the table. (See Illustration 72.) The base of this table is 14 inches high, to serve also as a coffee table. You may wish to play chess at standard table height, 28 inches.

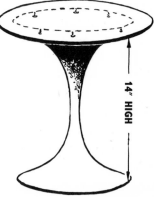

Illus. 72. The pedestal-shaped base for the table.

14″ HIGH

Illus. 73. *The Royal Game was never before played with pieces like these.*

Chessmen

Paste four quarter-sheets of paper. Tear in one inch strips.
Make little rolled sticks for armatures as follows:

2 Kings—2 5-inch sticks

2 Queens—2 4½-inch sticks

4 Bishops—4 4-inch sticks

4 Knights—4 4½-inch sticks

4 Rooks or castles—4 3-inch strips

16 Pawns—16 1½-inch strips

The pieces will be of different heights and thicknesses, but will be built in exactly the same way except for the head which identifies the piece. The horse's head of the knight is made by bending down one inch of the stick and fastening in place with a one-thickness strip of paper to hold it till it is dry.

Dry the sticks on a baking sheet. Sort out the sticks in rows in this and all the following procedures. This will save you time in sorting later. Work

Illus. 74. Making papier mâché chessmen.

with the baking sheet in front of you and place each piece back on the sheet in the same place after you have worked on it.

Build the base on each piece with mash, punching a border around the lower ¾ inch. Press a lead weight into the bottom of each and make sure that the bottom is concave, so the chess piece will not rock.

Bake the pieces on the baking sheet, standing them up in a normal position.

Build the heads on all the pawns: make a little round ball, roll it in the palms of your hands and stick on to the head of the stick.

Build the tops of all the major pieces, then bake them all in the oven. Cover the shank of the pieces between the top and the base with mash. Bake again.

The reason for baking between steps is a good one: The pieces are much easier to handle if you can hold them firmly without damaging a part you have already completed.

Dye half of your pieces black (16 in all, half of each type), and half Chinese red.

Apply one coat of clear lacquer and give the table one coat of lacquer.

Mix a package of cerise fabric dye and dip all the chess pieces, standing them on layers of paper to drain. Apply the cerise dye to the chess table with a brush and wipe off any excess with a cloth.

Four to ten more coats of clear lacquer finishes a chess table on which succeeding generations of your family can learn to play the Royal Game.

79

NATIVITY SCENE

Illus. 75.

The Nativity scene is a classic subject that has been reproduced by master artists and primitive artists all over the world.

This scene was made small, but it can be made as large as you wish, for the figures are light in weight and easy to handle.

Materials Checklist

stack of newspapers
flour and powdered resin glue mixture
wire (stranded picture hanging wire)
mash

This scene is built on the scale of one-half inch to the foot, making the male figures about 3 inches tall, Mary about 2½, the Baby Jesus about 1¼. The lambs' bodies are about one inch long, the ox 2½ inches, the donkey 2 inches. The manger is 2 inches long, the peak of the roof 6 inches high, the floor plan 6 x 3½ inches. The trees are 6 and 8 inches tall.

The Human Figures

There are nine human figures of adult size.

1. Paste four one-quarter sheets together.

2. Tear into strips one inch or less wide and about 5 inches long.

3. Paste four more one-quarter sheets together. Tear into 1 x 5 inch strips.

4. Roll each strip tightly lengthwise to make a "stick" measuring about $\frac{1}{8}$ inch by 5 inches.

5. Take two 5 inch sticks and one half of a stick and bind them together to make the head, two arms and two legs of the skeleton armature. (See Illustration 76.)

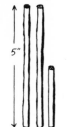 

5"

Illus. 76. Making a skeleton armature.

6. Bend arms, hands, feet, legs and head into position for the figure you are making, binding into position with one thickness of pasted paper. This paper may be torn off after the figure has been set by baking.

7. Bake on a baking sheet, setting the figures into the position they will take.

8. Tear off the binding strips. Add mash to body, head, hair, beards, hands, and legs and arms where they are to show. The shoulders should be built up to two heads wide, sloping down to the beginning of the arms. The costumes drape from the shoulders, so the shoulders must be modelled whether they are to show or not.

Faces are only indicated by pushing in the eye cavity, half way from top to bottom of the face. The nose ridge is made by pinching the space between the eyes with your thumb and first finger, tipping off the lower end to make it one-third the length of the whole face.

9. Bake to a tan; take the Mary figure out of the oven earlier and leave one of the kings in a little longer.

Clothing

1. Paste two one-quarter sheets together.

2. The basic garment of this biblical time and place is the tunic, a simple shift, short for the shepherds, and of floor length for the other figures. Tear a strip as wide as the shoulders and then tear it in half lengthwise, placing the middle of each strip on the shoulder. Drape into position, adding for some a tiny strip of twisted or flat paper for a belt. Sleeves are made with tiny pieces of paper folded around the arms.

3. Bake very lightly until dry and not brown.

4. Fill the bottom of cone made by tunic with mash.

Mary

When Mary's skeleton is made, also make a rock the right height for her to sit upon and fasten it to the figure.

For her headdress, tear a tiny triangle, one side of which is about $1\frac{1}{2}$ inches long. Place the middle of one side under her chin and draw it up around her face to the top of her head. Tear a 9 x 1 inch strip of single thickness pasted paper. Bring it through, over one arm and then up over her shoulders to the top of her head, about half way back. Drape it down over to the other arm and let it fall sidewise on to the floor one-quarter inch or so. Tear off any excess length. This garment is called a "himation" and was worn by women as an outer garment.

Joseph

Joseph's headdress is a one inch by $1\frac{1}{2}$ inch rectangle, placed at midforehead, smoothed back to cover the back of the head and shoulders, fastened with a paper cord worn straight around the head. His outer garment is made just like his under-tunic, but left open at the sides and with no sleeves. It is made wider and looser and bound with a twisted cord. His hand has been extended at the correct height and angle to touch Mary's shoulder.

Kings

One king has a coat with extra width and very wide sleeves. He is carrying a tiny jar, made from mash, as his gift. The crown is a circle. The king with the turban has a very narrow tunic and a narrow train with scallops at the

Illus. 77. Detail of the
Three Kings.

end. His gift is a tiny round box. His turban is made of a one inch by 5 inch strip of paper wrapped directly on the head.

The third king has a wider robe. His crown is a circle, with a high point cut with scissors before the circle was made. The box is folded paper, with a handle on top made of mash.

The Angel

The wings are added to the shoulder blades of the angel figure after it is dressed. These are four thicknesses of pasted paper; torn edges on the back edge indicate feathers.

The angel is hung from above with sewing thread of the same color as the background.

Baby Jesus

The Baby Jesus in this Nativity scene has no clothing, as in many of the classical paintings. It would be easier to make just the head and a one to $1\frac{1}{4}$ inch tube of wrapped strips to simulate the swaddling clothes mentioned in the biblical story. These should later be painted white.

Illus. 78.   Detail of the manger.

The Manger

1. Tear a 2 x 4 inch rectangle from four layers of pasted paper.

2. Fold in half and bind to the V-shaped trough. Make legs of folded paper and fasten two into an X-shape at each end.

The Halos for the Holy Family

Using very fine wire, make a circle about the size of the head. Bend about an inch of wire down at right angles to the halo; push the end of the wire down inside the clothing at the back of the neck while the costume is still wet for Mary, Joseph, and the angel; the Baby Jesus' halo is fastened at the head of the manger.

Bake all the costumed figures only until dry so they will not be too dark to paint with water-color.

Animals

1. Make "sticks" as for the human figures and make the skeletons of the animals, binding into position.

2. Bake.

3. Add mash to form the bodies.

4. Bake donkey and lambs only until dry; do not allow them to brown. The grey of the mash makes a perfect color for them. Bake the ox to a deep, rich brown.

Trees

Cut seven lengths of stranded picture wire, two 9 inches long, two 10 inches, two 11 inches, and one 12 inches.

For one tree use three strands, twisting the three together to make the trunk, about one-third of the way from the bottom end. Make the roots fairly long but rather flat. In real life, the roots of a tree are often as big as the tree, but a 4 to 5 inch spread would be good for the roots.

Keep separating and bending the wires to get smaller and smaller towards the ends of the branches or roots, just the way they grow.

Make the other tree from the four wires left. It is best not to make all of the trees the same size.

(The trees are the only thing in the book not made of papier mâché.)

The Stable

1. Make the stones of mash into little rectangles, one dimension always to be one-half inch. Make them as flat as can be, long, short, but always keep one side one-half inch thick.

2. Make a 6 x 3½ inch floor of four thicknesses of pasted paper.

3. Place a thin layer of mash about one-half inch wide around three edges of the floor.

4. Place a row of stones around the three sides, mash between each.

5. Make the second row, always choosing stones that overlap the joint in the previous layer.

6. When making the third row, place a long stone (about 1½ inches) at the middle of the back for a window sill.

7. Build up the rows three more layers, leaving the window about one inch wide.

8. On the edges of the window opening, build an arch, four stones on each side, curving slightly inward. Make a triangular block of wet mash for a keystone, and fit it into the top to make the curved window opening.

9. Continue to build until the side walls are 3½ inches high. Then build up the back wall to make a triangular gable 6 inches from the floor.

10. Make a pillar of stones up the middle front, 6 inches high.

11. Make a roof beam of rolled paper, 3½ inches long and fasten it to the pillar and the point of the back roof with mash.

12. Make the roof four thicknesses of pasted paper thick, tearing it to measure 4 x 8 inches, and fastening it to the roof beam and walls with mash. Tear narrow strips of colored paper in grey and yellow, and glue in random layers for a thatched roof.

Bake the stable in the oven, being careful not to brown the stones.

Painting

The faces and hands of all the figures have been toasted to the right color and do not need painting. Eyes and mouths were not even painted in. You can paint the costumes with tempera paints. Here are the shades used in the scene in the photograph.

The drapery around Mary's face is painted white. Her under-tunic is medium cobalt blue, her himation lighter blue.

Joseph's robe is blue green over a brown tunic, his headdress raw sienna.

The angel has a very light sea green tunic, streaks of blue and white in the wings.

The king with the turban has a purple robe, with highlights of red violet. His turban is brilliant red violet with little shadings of purple. His train is bluish purple. He has two stripes of brilliant red violet on his collar.

The king who carries the box wears red orange striped with brilliant red violet. The crown is raw sienna. The box has a raw sienna background with red-orange crosshatching; a little purple dot is in each square; a scalloped circle in red-orange decorates the top.

The king with the big sleeves has a jade green robe. His tunic has red and purple spots. There is a lime and yellow panel on the front and back of his tunic. He carries a tiny orange jar.

One of the shepherds has a purple and black striped tunic, another has one of black and tan stripes, and the last has one of mottled grey and tan.

The animals need no painting at all. They were baked to just the right color.

6. Drying the Things You Make

BAKING

If a piece can be designed so that it can be baked in the oven, drying will be quicker. An oven can be an important piece of equipment.

Most wastebaskets will be too large to be baked in an oven. If you are working in a group, someone may have access to a hotel or restaurant oven, or a nearby school or church may have a large size oven that you can use.

The hot sun will dry anything quickly. Use an aluminium sun reflector or an aluminium painted roof top to intensify the temperature. Leave the papier mâché drying in the sun long after it is dry.

Two hundred and fifty degrees is the ideal heat for baking in the oven. It makes a better, harder product. Use an oven thermometer.

For large pieces or large quantities of papier mâché, convert a closet or a small room to a dryer. Line the room completely with aluminium foil. (This intensifies the heat for the drying of your papier mâché.)

Anything will dry naturally in an ordinary room with ordinary heat. But the air can get a bit damp if you are making several pieces. And the damper the air gets, the slower they will dry. It is just nice to get them dry, checked, surfaced and finished so that you can enjoy them. Then you can go ahead and use the space to make some more things.

Of course things will dry naturally without any special drying arrangements, but the drying process takes longer.

There may be some warping each time you bake your piece. Provide for it in your design. Some papers and glues will warp more than others. But it is the nature of papier mâché to warp, so take advantage of this to give your work individuality. Do not try to copy pottery or wood or machine-made mass-produced plastic or metal.

Warping will not happen if your piece is dried on the mould. Give it a finish coat immediately after it is dry. Warping does not take place either when there is very high humidity.

7. Decorating the Things You Make

Many of the pieces you make will look just right with a minimum of decoration, even though the texture of papier mâché is often decorative enough in itself. Part of the charm of papier mâché lies in the fact that you can achieve textures that cannot be obtained with other materials.

There may be times, however, when you will want to add something to the natural texture. One technique is collage—this can be used to advantage on objects made by the pasted strip method. The wastepaper baskets shown in Illustration 79 were decorated in this way. The trays shown in Illustration 18 are also decorated with collages. By definition, collage is nothing more than the application of cut out or torn designs, forms or materials to an object. They can be entire photographs or drawings, stamps, pages from an old book or from advertisements in a popular magazine, motifs from wallpaper—the list is seemingly endless. These are simply pasted on the object before the final finish is applied. You are not limited to complete subjects, either. Experiment with tearing strips and shapes of color from advertisements—in effect, to "paint" your designs with bits of colored paper.

To make a "palette" of colors, begin by collecting a pile of magazines. Ask your friends to save them for you. Tear out all of the pages that have pictures that interest you or colors that might be useful. When you have collected a large supply of pages, sort them out into file folders or shirt boxes. Place the pictures and illustrations in one file; in the others, sort out the blocks of color, labelling the files "Red," "Yellow," "Blue," "Green," etc. Discard any pastel colors below a medium value and any greyed tones. You will be surprised at the range you can collect. If you need designs of fruit for decoration, for example, you will want plenty of lemon yellow, banana yellow, apple red, etc.

PUNCHING, OR INCISING

Mash lends itself to quite another decorating technique—the punching or incising of designs into the surface of the semi-solid mash. Use "tools" that exist in the home—in kitchen, desk drawers, sewing box or dressing table: pencils, pieces of dowelling, buttons, hairpins.

The mash must be quite stiff. Water content makes the mash shrink a good bit in drying, so the design becomes less defined.

Lay the mash on thickly enough so you can draw lines deep enough to make a dark, sharp shadow. Lay the mash on evenly enough, too, so that all the holes will be about the same depth. A one-quarter inch depth works well.

If holes are punched too close together, each will distort the next. Sometimes this can give a good effect, but if you don't like what you have done, smooth it over and start again.

Measuring the distance between each punch should be done only with the eye. In making a border, punch a hole at each end, then one in the middle, then in the middle of each side until you have as many as you want. If they are a bit off, your effect will still be more pleasing than if made by machine.

Collect all the things that you think might be interesting as tools. Place them on a tray near you.

Place your piece to be decorated in front of you on clean papers on the baking sheet, so it can be moved without handling it. Cover it with one-quarter inch of mash.

Place a container of water beside you. If the tool sticks to the mash when you press it in, and draws some of the mash back out with it, dip the tool in the water and press the mash into the space again. The whole surface must be incised within a few hours, before a skin begins to form on the surface.

Dyes and water-colors are excellent for coloring mash-coated objects—either as the ground color for over-all decoration or for the background color upon which other designs will be laid on. Use batik, fabric, leather, furniture or food dyes. Some of these may be available in alcohol-soluble or water-soluble types. The water-soluble dyes are simpler and more desirable to use.

For small papier mâché objects, use artists' tube or pan-type water-colors.

The advantage of dyes and water-colors over opaque pigments and paints is that they allow the texture of the papier mâché to show through.

A subsequent covering of epoxy, lacquer, or other finish will protect the surface.

8. Finishes for the Things You Make

Up until now, you have finished some of your projects with simple and quick-drying materials like brushing lacquer. There are other materials that can be used, some of which are more desirable for objects made by the strip method and others which are better for the mash objects.

The only thing to remember in applying any finish is that many thin coats are more desirable than a few thick ones. It is especially important that the first coats be thin; later coats can be thicker if you want to speed up the finishing process.

Strip method objects are decorated with opaque finishes to disguise the newspaper printing, unless you cover by the collage technique. There are circumstances when you might want the decoration to be pieces of newspaper: Suppose that on a trip abroad you collected newspapers in every country you visited. Pieces of such newspaper showing datelines and news stories applied to a tray or large bowl would make a wonderful souvenir of your trip. In this case, of course, a clear finish would be dictated.

LINSEED OIL

Many of the projects in this book have specified that the objects be coated or soaked with raw linseed oil and baked. These directions are based on old recipes for papier mâché, and they are important. Papier mâché articles that have been given the linseed oil treatment before baking are impervious to water. They tend, too, to be harder and stronger than articles that have not received such treatment. Where strength and durability are considerations, you should always treat your papier mâché articles with linseed oil before baking them.

You may occasionally find that paint suppliers do not have raw linseed oil available. In that event, you can substitute boiled linseed oil. The boiled oil is quicker drying, but both respond to baking in the same way.

Illus. 79. These wastepaper baskets have been decorated using the collage technique described on page 88.

OPAQUE FINISHES

LACQUER: Colored brushing lacquers are widely available and are easy to handle. (Note: Brushing lacquers are to be preferred to the spraying type of lacquer.) As with many finishes, lacquer is best applied in thin coats that are allowed to dry between coats. (Lacquer dries quickly by the evaporation of the vehicle, which is highly volatile.) For an extremely high-gloss finish, the surface can be smoothed with fine emery paper between coats. The advantages of lacquer over other finishes are its ease of handling and its "rightness" for papier mâché. Lacquer not only looks right but is right on papier mâché. It has been the traditional finish for papier mâché objects for centuries.

PAINT: Ordinary oil-base and water-base paints can be used on papier mâché, but their use should be limited to emergencies when other materials like lacquer are not available. Tempera (water) colors can also be used, but because the real enemy of papier mâché is moisture, the best finishes are those that repel moisture. It is a false economy indeed to spend your time making a project, yet fail to protect what you have made with the proper materials.

TRANSPARENT FINISHES

LACQUER: Clear brushing lacquer is as widely available as the pigmented, opaque kind. As you may already have discovered when you made the papier mâché beads on page 34, it is simple and pleasant to work with. Small objects can be dipped repeatedly in thinned clear lacquer to give a quickly applied and attractive finish. More important, the dipping process is almost free of mess—there are no brushes to clean afterwards. If you use discarded food jars in which to do your dipping, the lacquer can be kept for use from project to project. Objects like large bowls and wastepaper baskets require that the finish be applied by brushing. You can only discover the pleasures of working with lacquer by using it. Unlike paint and varnish, which seem to lie on the surface, succeeding coats of lacquer blend into under-coats. If you find that one coat has left annoyingly apparent brush marks, you can cover them up by blending them in on the next coat. TIP: The thinner the lacquer the easier it is to blend. (Use lacquer thinner to dilute it, adding more thinner at intervals to make up for the solvent lost by evaporation.)

SHELLAC: Here is another relatively quick-drying finish that you can use to advantage on certain pieces. On papier mâché, shellac has a soft "feel" and, like lacquer, it is taken up in part by the papier mâché instead of lying on the surface. Shellac comes in clear (white) and orange types; use the white shellac for most finishes, but experiment with orange shellac if you want some interesting antique effects. Always thin shellac to a water-like consistency with denatured alcohol.

Unfortunately, shellac does not make a good finish on objects that are to be exposed to alcohol or water. A shellac-coated papier mâché surface would soon be marred if glasses were set on it; shellac would be an inappropriate finish for coasters of papier mâché or for a table covered in papier mâché. Water causes a whitish "bloom" to appear on shellac-covered surfaces; this bloom seems to persist even after the surface is dry. Nevertheless, because of its wide availability and ease of application, shellac should be considered as an appropriate finish for many surfaces.

VARNISH: In the days of sailing ships, varnish was widely used to coat the decks, masts and spars; it still finds wide application in maritime uses today where its imperviousness to moisture makes it a necessity. Generally speaking, though, varnish has little usefulness in papier mâché. Its tendency to lie on the surface of a piece like a thick skin or integument (rather than being taken up in part by the papier mâché) and its rather lengthy drying time (varnish dries by oxidation, rather than evaporation) make it the least desirable finish. If you have an application requiring the special qualities of varnish, you should use it. If you are making architectural panels of papier mâché intended to be exposed to the weather, of course varnish would be an ideal finish.

LIQUID EPOXY: Epoxy resins have proven to be the wonder children of modern chemistry. Various liquid epoxy finishes are now available in clear and colored (pigmented) form. These are marketed in two containers, one containing the epoxy resin and the other the hardener. The two components are not combined until you are ready to use the resulting liquid epoxy finish.

It has been found that an object coated with epoxy can be bent repeatedly until it breaks, yet the coating will not chip, crack or break. Epoxy resins have been used as adhesives in special applications, such as the fabrication of giant aircraft, and epoxy resins will hold two parts together better than will rivets. Two pieces of material joined with epoxy resins will break before the joint will give way.

Such unusual properties can have some exciting applications in papier mâché work. When you make an object where strength is a requisite, coat it with a liquid epoxy product and you will find that you have created something practically indestructible. Be certain to use epoxy to coat wastepaper baskets, furniture and architectural panels.

In working with epoxy products, follow the instructions supplied with the product and observe the following precautionary measures:

Contact with the skin and eyes must be avoided. Use rubber gloves on your hands and do not touch your skin if the gloves come in contact with the epoxy finish while it is wet. Ventilate the room with a fan.

If skin contact occurs, wash the affected part (but not the eyes) with alcohol, followed by a thorough rinsing with soap and water.

9. Projects for Damp Days

There will be times when all of your projects have been made and are in the process of drying—and aren't drying quickly because the day is damp and rainy. This is a good time to make some useful accessories for your papier mâché work. Here are a couple of useful items to make your mixing and finishing quicker and easier:

WHISK

A whisk for mixing paste and casein glue is useful and will cost you nothing but two coat hangers and a few minutes' time.

Materials Checklist

2 light-weight coat hangers

Take each of the two coat hangers. Bend them in half, then tightly together at the top (hooked end). Spread to 3 inches at the bottom end.

Twist one hook tightly around the other to fasten the two hangers together. (See Illustration 80.)

SUPPORTS FOR DRYING

Make supports like these when you want to finish a papier mâché object by dipping it.

Materials Checklist

four pieces of $\frac{1}{4}$ inch plywood, each 3 inches square
four 1 inch long box nails

Nail a box nail right through the middle of each square of plywood. The piece to be dried simply rests on these points; the points of the nails will not mark the object that is being dried. For a large number of small pieces, nail many nails through a large piece of $\frac{1}{4}$ inch plywood so that it looks like a Hindu fakir's bed of nails. (See Illustration 81.)

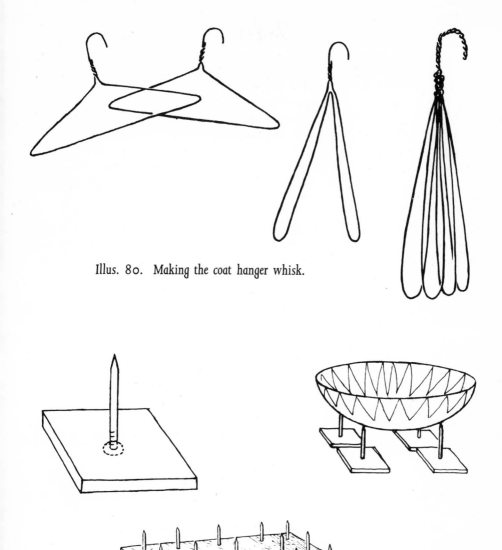

Illus. 80. Making the coat hanger whisk.

Illus. 81. Making supports for drying.

Index

Art of working with mash, 45
Baking, 87
Beads, 34
Blinds, 39
Blocks, children's building, 47
Bowl, round, 48
  salad, 17
Box, file, 9
  tool, 68
  toy, 53
Boxes, hat, 32
  rectangular, 54
Buttons, 37
Cache-pots, 50
Candle holders, 47
Candlesticks, 72
Canisters, 60
Cherubs and figurines, 43
Chess table and chessmen, 75
Children's building blocks, 47
Child's stool and toy box, 53
Cleansing tissue box cover, 52
Clock case, 70
Collage, 88
Cylindrical lampshades, 24
Decorating the things
  you make, 88
Dish, nut, 10
Drying, supports for, 94
  the things you make, 87
Dyes, 89
Epoxy, liquid, 93
Figurines, 43
File box, 9
Finishes for the things you
  make, 90

opaque, 91
  transparent, 92
Flower pot covers, 50
Folded and rolled objects, 34
Fork, salad, 19
Funnels, 65
Getting acquainted with papier
  mâché, 8
Glues, 7
Grain of paper, 6
Hat boxes, 32
Incising, 88
Introduction, 5
Lacquer, 91, 92
Lampshades, 24, 69
Linseed oil, 90
Liquid epoxy, 93
Mash, how to make, 45
Materials, of papier mâché, 6, 7
Moulds, 8
Napkin rings, 51
Nativity scene, 80
Nut dish, 10
Opaque finishes, 91
Paint, 91
Panels, 67
Paper, 6
Papier mâché, definition of, 5
  raw materials of, 6
Paste, wallpaper, 24
Pastes and glues, 7
Pencil cups, 58
Projects for damp days, 94
Punching, or incising, 88
Puppet heads, 71
Putting your skills to work, 23

Raw materials of papier
  mâché, 6
Rectangular boxes with lids
  and lips, 54
Rectangular trays, 27, 28
Rolled objects, 34
Round bowl, 48
  trays, 26
  wastepaper basket, 23
Salad bowl, 17
Salad fork and serving
  spoon, 19
Sectional shelves, 30
Shakers, 63
Shellac, 92
Shelves, sectional, 30
Spice and condiment
  canisters, 60
Spoon, serving, 19
Stool, child's, 53
Strip method, 10
Supports for drying, 94
Table, chess, 75
Tool box, 68
Toy box, 53
Transparent finishes, 92
Trays, rectangular, 27, 28
  round, 26
Varnish, 92
Wallpaper paste, 24
Wastepaper basket, round, 23
  woven, 41
Water-colors, 89
Whisk, 46, 94
Woven wastepaper baskets, 41